Chapters

D1521071

Chapter 1

My First Try

Back in my younger days, a co-worker, Rob, told me a story about his most memorable experience umpiring Little League baseball in his home state of Missouri.

In one game, Rob squatted behind the catcher to call balls and strikes. Then it happened. The pitcher fired a pitch, the batter swung, and the ball was fouled straight back at Rob, who fell to his knees in shock and pain after the ball hit him in his throat. Down on his knees, coughing and gagging, all Rob could hear were some fans clapping, with one loudmouth sarcastically blurting out, "Nice catch, ump!"

Years later, when he told me the story as a grown man, Rob, a gifted story-teller, made this incident sound strangely serious and humorous at the same time. At the time it happened as a younger man, though, Rob wasn't in a laughing mood. That was the last summer that he umpired baseball.

As I listened to Rob tell this story, the thought that went through my mind was that I would never want to umpire baseball, softball or anything else that included balls and strikes, bats and uniforms, and fans in the stands.

Who would want to go through all that hassle? Who would want to take all that abuse? Who would want to be heckled and laughed at by fans?

Well, I guess the answer is me. I do.

Little did I know that while in my mid-30s, several years after listening to Rob's ball-to-the-throat story, I would become an umpire in Midland, Michigan.

I first decided to give it a try after another one of my co-workers, Ted, told me that he was umpiring slow-pitch softball as a way to make extra money. In the mid-1990s, umpires were paid $18 a game in the Midland recreation leagues, and it was possible to umpire three or four games a night during the week.

I was newly married at the time, so a little extra money wasn't going to hurt. In the summer of 1995, I signed up to umpire with the Midland Parks and Recreation Department.

I umpired slow pitch games for men and women. I umpired all adult levels of play. I also umpired church leagues. During that era, it should be noted that the two most challenging groups to umpire were the 50-and-over players and the church league players.

The senior players thought they knew everything and could say anything. They would joke and laugh in the dugout, and then they would provoke the umpires with a biting comment.

The church players, for some reason, seemed to think that every game was Game 7 of the World Series. They took matters very seriously. Their games were edgy. Not every church league was like this. It seemed as though the more competitive the league, the more issues an umpire had with the players and coaches.

In my first season of umpiring slow-pitch, the closest that I ever came to ejecting someone was when a church team coach raced out of the dugout to argue a call. He was very demonstrative. He did not use foul language, but he was acting unsportsmanlike, waving his arms and yelling loudly. My sin? I had called one of his base runners out at the plate on a close play.

During incidents like this, you are tempted to ask the team, "What church do you attend? I'll make sure to never go there."

For two summers, I umpired slow-pitch softball. I would race home from work, eat a quick dinner, and be off to the diamonds, usually arriving to the field at 5:30 for a 6 o'clock game.

If a person kept this schedule two, three or four times a week, it could eventually wear you down --- even someone in their 30s, like me at the time. After all the games were completed at night, I would arrive back at home between 10 to midnight, depending on how many games I had worked.

The majority of the time, I was exhausted. Due to the fact that I had a full-time job as a sportswriter at the local newspaper, I had to be at work early the next morning. The schedule was a struggle and I rarely had any down time.

Softball season started in early May, and by late July, my attitude would begin to sour. Exhaustion led to negativity. Negative thoughts and a bad attitude started to overcome me as I was driving to the games. That is never a good sign with any job, much less umpiring and dealing with competitive people on a ball diamond.

In a peculiar kind of way, I felt myself almost being eager to deal with conflict so I could release my frustration. My patience was very thin by the end of July. I knew it, and I believe that some of the softball players knew it as well.

I never threw anyone out of a game, but I started to verbally respond more instead of just letting the players and coaches vent at me. I tried to be patient and to be approachable, but my tolerance level was fading quickly by the end of summer.

So, at the end of my second summer of umpiring, I decided that I was done. Yes, the money was nice, but I was wearing myself out, and I was not enjoying myself anymore. My attitude was such that I felt I needed a break. I did not enjoy going to the ballpark. A seven-inning game seemed like it dragged on for five hours.

I took a break from umpiring after that summer for the next 14 years.

In 2010, when I turned 50, I decided to return to umpiring. My life circumstances changed. I now was the father of two young daughters, and I wanted to get back in the game. Sure, I was older and slower, but I also was wiser, much more patient and determined to put forth my best effort.

This time, I had a whole new challenge on my hands. I decided to umpire youth and high school girls' fast-pitch.

Chapter 2

Back in the game

The first thing that I noticed when I decided to return to umpiring was that there is a big difference between being 36 and being 50. At 36, I was in the best shape of my life after having dropped close to 40 pounds. I was playing lunch-time basketball three times a week, eating a very strict diet and exercising on a regular basis.

At 50, I was officially in middle-age years, and now the father of two young girls. My hair was turning white, power naps were part of my daily routine, my eating habits were pretty shoddy, and my stomach was regrettably expanding. Other strange things started happening to my maturing body, as well.

I was most certainly not as quick or as flexible as I was at 36. Not even close. As it is said, Father Time is undefeated. I was also not as quick to recover after a long day of being on the field, standing on my feet and having to umpire a seven-inning game.

That's just the physical side of the job. The financial part also was an eye-opener.

The out-of-pocket money to get started is much more expensive in fast-pitch. I spent well over six hundred dollars for my gear, which included shin guards, mask, shoes, chest protector, etc., and uniforms for both high school and youth spring and summer games. I also had to pay to register with the various umpires associations, and to attend certain clinics to get educated on the craft.

After a while, I was beginning to wonder, "Are they paying me or am I paying them?"

By the time I had umpired my first high school game, I had spent at least seven hundred dollars. It would take a lot of games to work to break even. For this reason, the veteran umpires like to tell the rookie umpires, "Don't do this for the money."

This is the bottom line: You end up spending a lot of money to umpire fast-pitch softball. It is not just the gear and the uniforms. Other expenses include the food, gas money, clinic and association fees, buying ice for the cooler - or buying a new cooler. The expenses all add up. One year that I recall, I spent roughly one thousand dollars on clothes, food, gas, equipment and other items. When I went to my accountant the next spring to do my taxes, my income and my expenditures (including mileage) were just about a wash. I broke even.

Truthfully, a person really needs to have a strong passion to be an umpire. Sure, some umpires do it only for the money. The pay is roughly eighty to one hundred ten dollars for a high school doubleheader in Michigan. Others do it because they love it and to them getting paid is an added benefit.

I believe that I do it because I love it. Sure, I may complain about the chilly spring weather or a hostile coach, but the truth is that it is fun. I love the competition, the camaraderie among umpires, and the feeling of being in charge and enforcing the rules.

The pay certainly is a nice bonus. I cannot complain. On average, I typically make twenty-four to twenty-eight dollars an hour, depending on how quickly the games go in high school.

One time, I umpired a junior varsity doubleheader that ended in only two hours because the teams were extremely unevenly matched. I was paid eighty dollars for the two games, which averaged out to forty dollars an hour.

The pay sure is better than working at Home Depot for a part-time job, earning about ten dollars an hour and having to lift bags of top soil or mulch for customers.

Chapter 3

The cup caper

The first year on a job is always a challenge. That is true if you are a bank teller, a brick layer, a chemist or an umpire.

Everything you experience, you're experiencing for the first time. There's a huge learning curve in most cases. Even though I had umpired slow-pitch several years prior, fast pitch at the youth and high school level was a whole new experience for me.

For one thing, this was my first time seeing softball pitchers throw hard while I was behind the plate. No blinking allowed. The game, obviously, was much quicker than slow-pitch. I had to adjust to the game the best way that I could.

I received a fair amount of junior varsity and club assignments that spring. Understandably, the person who was in charge of assigning games, fittingly called the assignor, did not allow rookies to umpire high school varsity games because it is not fair to the new umpire, or to the teams. The umpire has to learn everything from processing information to dealing with lineup changes to enforcing rules. There is a tremendous amount of information to absorb.

In my first year, I had to "pay my dues." I always umpired junior varsity games, some of which were very poorly played. I drove as far as forty-five miles to umpire at a school in a rural area, probably because no one else wanted the assignment. I did it because turning down games was never a good thing, especially in your first year. You don't want to earn that reputation, because it may cost you future assignments.

I accepted all of the games that I was assigned because I knew that was what was best for me at this point in my young umpiring career.

One of my assignments during that first year was for a one-umpire job in Hemlock, a small farming community in mid-Michigan that takes softball very seriously. A youth game might attract as many as one hundred fans, which included lots of parents along with grandmas, grandpas, cousins and neighbors.

It was a beautiful, early summer day when I arrived at the park for an age 13-and-under game. Typically, I park my vehicle, a Chevy Trail Blazer, away from fans and the field so I have privacy and I don't feel compelled to interact with spectators, players or coaches. In this case, I decided to park it near some woods, about 30 yards behind the diamond's backstop.

I always got my chair out of the vehicle first, so I had something to sit on. From there, I got into my gear --- shoes, shin guards, chest protector. I made sure that I had my indicator to call balls and strikes, and a pencil or pen to write on the lineup cards.

Before I left for the field, I did a self-check and went through my entire list of items and gear, from head to toe – pen, indicator, plate brush, lineup cards, supportive cup, etc. Don't laugh. A few male umpires have told me that they have forgotten to put on their cup, and ended up racing back to their car before a game to put it on.

As this game in Hemlock progressed, I noticed that my cup just wasn't feeling right. Something was a bit off, and I was feeling uncomfortable. When I would move out from behind the plate, my cup was moving a bit too much for my liking. I couldn't readjust it the way I needed to -- not with all these parents and players watching me. Most assuredly, I wasn't going to call a time-out to run into the woods. That would have been embarrassing.

I just had to live with it.

Then, the third inning arrived.

A batter stepped into the box. The catcher signaled to the pitcher. The pitcher threw the pitch and the batter swung the bat. The ball went to the outfield, and as I sprung out of my position from behind the plate to get a better view of the ball, I felt something start to slowly slide down my left pant-leg.

It was my cup.........

Immediately, I figured that everyone was going to be watching the ball and the base runner, so I had a split decision to make. I could follow the ball and do my umpiring duties. Or, I could grab my cup before anyone could see what had happened, including the catcher. I chose my cup, which was now cozied up near home plate.

With no one noticing (at least, I hope that was the case), I quickly scooped up my cup and put it in my ball bag. It stayed there for the remainder of the game. I was very cautious for the duration of the game whenever I got behind the catcher. I would put my hands down with fists clenched to guard my private area from possible harm.

For the next forty-five minutes or so, I had never prayed so hard in my life that the pitchers would be pinpoint accurate and the catchers would be like brick walls for the rest of the game.

They performed wonderfully. Prayers answered.

A few years later, after I had umpired many more games, I did something that I thought I would never, ever do as an umpire.

During a Saturday tournament in Coleman, another small community that loves softball, I worked two games – with a long break between the two. I was assigned the championship game, but it seemed like it took forever for it to start because of the length of the previous games being played.

I was eager and antsy as I waited impatiently in my vehicle. I got in and out of my Trail Blazer about a dozen times to check on the status of the games being played. When the championship game finally was about to begin, I called over to my partner, "Let's get this thing started as quickly as possible."

We briskly walked to the field. As the plate umpire, I rushed through the managers' meeting at home plate, and I told the teams that we were ready to start. I was all business. No smiling, no small talk. I was eager to get it started because I had already waited so long.

One pitch was thrown to the plate, then another, then another. The game was off to a fast start.

Since it was a bright, sunny day, I needed to adjust my sunglasses, so I went to remove my mask. As I went to grasp my mask and remove it, I quickly discovered that I did not have my mask on my head.

I had completely forgotten it. I just about croaked.

Totally ashamed and embarrassed, I frantically called time out and raced to my vehicle about 40 yards away to get my mask. Fans, I'm certain, were puzzled about what I was doing. I can't even imagine what the players were thinking. Maybe they thought I was sick or that someone was stealing something from my vehicle and I was chasing them down.

When I got back to the field, huffing and puffing, one of the coaches slowly approached me and quietly asked, "How could you forget your mask?"

I had no answer. I was tired. I was a bit angry. I was in a hurry. I was mentally in La-La Land. In a nutshell, that sums up why I did what I did.

Lesson learned: Always go through a self-check on your equipment to avoid 40-yard sprints to start a ball game. Otherwise, you could take a foul-tip right in the nose.

Chapter 4

Hot buttons

After my first year of umpiring fast-pitch softball, I attended an Amateur Softball Association (now called USA Softball) state clinic, which umpires are encouraged to attend in order to fine-tune their skills in the off-season.

These day-long clinics usually take place in the late winter or early spring, a few weeks before the high school season begins in the Michigan High School Athletic Association. To become an ASA umpire, a person is required to pass a 50-question test, which includes true-false scenarios and multiple choice questions. A score of 70 percent is required to pass.

At the state clinic, a variety of topics are covered. These topics include everything from positioning on the bases and behind the plate to various rules, with a strong emphasis on obstruction and interference. Obstruction is when the defensive player impedes the progress of the offensive player, while interference is when the offensive player interferes with the defensive player. Sometimes those rules and terms get confused.

There were also hour-long classroom sessions to go along with practice work in the gym. The day is pretty intense. By the time it concludes late in the afternoon, participants are tired and ready to head home.

I attended one classroom session for rookie and second- and third-year umpires. The person who led this session shared a piece of wisdom that I have never forgotten. It was simple, but very insightful.

He was a veteran umpire, probably in his late 50s, who had witnessed his share of difficult situations over the years. He warned us that we needed to be prepared to face uncomfortable situations and difficult people at all times on this job. He told us that it all starts with self-awareness.

This is what he said that has stuck with me to this day: Know what your hot buttons are, and protect them. That was an excellent piece of advice, not only for umpiring, but also for marriage, relationships at work and dealing with your kids or neighbors. An umpire must be aware of his or her vulnerable areas.

He shared an example of an umpire who had served time in prison. This new umpire was trying to get his life in order, and that is why he had decided to ump. One of the teams in the league found out that he had been convicted of a crime and spent time in prison, so players on this team made his life very difficult during one game by teasing him and saying mean things. They were relentless.

Finally, after hearing one too many comments, this umpire lost his temper and had to be restrained by his partner. He had reached his breaking point. His hot button had been pushed, and he exploded.

In order to survive in this business, no matter the level of competition, it is crucial to protect the vulnerable, emotional areas in your mind, which are also known as hot buttons. If they are left unguarded, bad things usually occur.

A personal example of this happened to me. Someone touched one of my hot buttons in a tournament game a few years ago. It was my fourth game of the night. I was tired and it was hot, and I let my guard down.

I had been telling players on each team to keep one foot in the batter's box when taking signals from the third base coach. This is a rule that helps the game to progress quickly.

As what typically happens in girls' softball, some players were following my direction and some were not. I was getting frustrated with the players who were stepping out of the box with both feet. After reaching my breaking point, I loudly told one player to, "keep one foot in the box."

The head coach of her team, who was in the third base coaching box, snapped at me. "If you tell our players that, you had better tell their players that."

A majority of the time, I would let a comment like that pass by. This time, it was different. That comment hit me the wrong way, and I snapped. "I've been telling both teams that the entire game," I yelled to the coach. Now, my blood was boiling. She didn't respond because she knew I was miffed. I slowly seethed for the rest of the game. It was not a good feeling.

When the game ended, I spent time thinking about that incident. Why did that coach's comment bother me so much? Why did I snap? Why couldn't I just brush off her comment?

My conclusion was that I had felt disrespected (a hot button for me). I also didn't feel like that coach had trusted me to do my job correctly and professionally. She had doubted me. This is another one of my hot buttons.

It was a perfect storm – her tone and words set me off, and my mental guard was down. That was a toxic combination. Looking back on it, I should have just started calling strikes on the batters who stepped out of the box with both feet. As an umpire, I have that authority. The rulebook would support me. That is another lesson I have learned. I chalked up that night as a chance to grow and mature as an umpire.

Moving forward, I knew I had to be more proactive in protecting my vulnerable areas, because that coach did get to me. It doesn't matter if the weather is hot, the day has been a long, or I'm dead on my feet. There should be no excuses. I need to be aware of my hot buttons if I want to be a good umpire.

In order to prepare myself for a game, especially ones that I knew were going to be very competitive, I routinely rehearsed in my mind plays and scenarios that I might encounter, and how I should deal with them. I did a lot of self-talk. If an illegal pitch is thrown, how should I respond? If a coach argues a call, how can I best exercise self-control? If the teams are not hustling on and off the field, what should I say and what should my tone be?

I would think through a game before it happened, and I listened to the advice of my fellow umpires.

For example, one veteran crew member, Dave, told me that I should keep my hands behind my back when a coach argues with me, specifically if I was working the bases. The body language translates into being approachable and willing to listen. Dave saw me with my arms crossed during one confrontation with a coach. That is why he gave me this advice.

Veteran umpires are typically more than willing to share their wisdom and advice, and it's up to inexperienced umpires to be willing to listen and learn.

Chapter 5

Partners

As an umpire, you partner with all kinds of people: young and old, male and female, experienced and inexperienced. One day your partner may be in their 70s and have been umpiring for 40 years, and the next day your partner may be in their early 20s, making their very first appearance on the diamond. This type of variable scheduling of umpire partners happens on a fairly routine basis.

In most cases, you just never know who you are going to be paired with until you see your game assignment.

I have had some memorable partners over the years. Some partners make you laugh and some make you angry. Some partners you click with so well, you wish they would be paired with you for every game until you retire from umpiring.

Umpire pairing varies throughout the spring and summer.

During one early-season high school doubleheader in April, I worked with a middle-aged female umpire who was not having a good day.

It was a cold and blustery April afternoon, and these games were horrible. This game was an example of junior varsity softball at its absolute worst.

Soon, my partner had reached her breaking point.

She was working behind the plate for the first game of the double header, and the score just kept getting more and more out of hand - 10-0, 15-2, 22-2. It was turning into a rout.

According to the rule book, after the third inning of high school ball, there is a fifteen-run "mercy rule". This means that the game can be ended by an umpire if one team is trailing the other by fifteen or more runs.

This first game of the double header was an example of this. The home team was trailing by 20 runs heading into the bottom of the third inning. That is when my partner had seen enough.

"That's it. This game is over," she yelled.

The problem was, the home team still needed to bat in order to complete the game. That also is the rule. The home team coach was baffled as to what was going on. "You can't call the game," she said to the home plate umpire, "we still need to bat."

By that time, my partner had hustled off the field and headed to her car to get out of her plate gear. She ignored the coach's plea. I was standing in the infield, debating what I should do. Should I go get my partner? Should I stay on the field?

I finally hurried to catch up with her to ask her what her thinking was. As home plate umpire, she is in charge of the game.

"They still need to bat," I said of the home team.

She quickly responded, "This game is over. There's no way they're going to catch up. Besides, it's just too cold to be out here this long."

Between the first and second games of the double header, I tried to make peace with the home team coach because I knew that the call was wrong. She was not happy and I didn't blame her. That was the wrong call to make by our crew. What transpired that afternoon bothered me throughout the night. The following day, I called the athletic director of the school to apologize. I wanted him to make sure that I had no part in that decision, and that I was just as frustrated with the call to end the game prematurely as his school's coach.

Here are a couple of other embarrassing situations on the diamond.

Before the start of a game, an umpire is encouraged to meet with his partner to make sure you both are in agreement about clearly communicating on the field. You may go over base coverage, or certain plays or situations, and you might go over signals. One such signal you may cover is communicating on the "infield fly rule," which comes into play when there are batters on first and second or on first, second and third, with fewer than two outs.

Early one Friday morning at the beginning of a three day tournament, I met my partner about an hour before our first game. He was about my age – early 50s. I was told by the tournament director that he was an experienced umpire, in fact, one of the best for this organization, so I was eager to work with him.

During our pre-game meeting, we talked about a number of rules, but I noticed that he just did not seem to be too interested in discussing the rules. He also was not too fond of proper mechanics and signals.

Typically, to communicate the infield fly situation, an umpire will put his right hand to the left side of his chest.

This is a quick motion because you want to discreetly get your partner's attention. It is just so you are on the same page.

When I brought this up with this particular partner, he was not interested in talking about it. He had his own agenda. He said that he may do the typical signal (hand to chest) or he might do something else. He then proceeded to act like King Kong, and pounded his chest with both fists.

I smiled because I thought that he was joking. I soon found out that it was not a joke.

Sure enough, in about the second or third inning, we had an infield fly situation. I was the base umpire, and I signaled to him – right hand to the left side of my chest. He then stepped out from behind the catcher, looked directly at me and pounded his chest with both fists. Fortunately, no Tarzan sounds accompanied his theatrics.

I could feel the embarrassment seeping through my body. I could have crawled underneath the third base bag. I was horrified.

We worked seven games together during that weekend tournament. Thankfully, that was the last time I ever saw him.

I was involved in another lopsided scoring high school game that turned ugly. This time, my partner was a young guy, probably in his early to mid-20s. He grew increasingly impatient as the score became more and more out of hand.

The home team was scoring run after run. They were hitting anything near the strike zone, and the other team's pitcher had little to no chance to get them out.

At this time, my partner, who was working behind the plate, decided to widen the strike zone a bit – to the size of a small mobile home. To widen it by a few inches is fine. As umpires, we all do that at times to get players to be more aggressive at the plate, particularly at the younger levels.

This was beyond ridiculous.

At one point, the pitcher threw a pitch that was ten feet above the batter's head, and he called it a strike. The ball hit the backstop, and my jaw nearly hit the infield dirt. I couldn't believe it, and neither could the batter.

The home team's first base coach was justifiably stunned. He looked at me, and said, "What's he doing?" I replied, "I have no idea."

I didn't want to throw my partner under the bus, although I vehemently disagreed with what he was doing.

My partner was very frustrated with the lopsided nature of the game. He wanted to get the game over, and he wanted batters to swing at every pitch -- even if the pitch was ten feet above their heads.

The day could not end soon enough for me.

Experiences like these make you appreciate the good umpires in youth and high school softball. There are scores of men and women who care, act professionally, put the time in to train and prepare, and who want to do their best at each and every game.

I know that I have come to appreciate conscientious umpires more and more. That is especially true after having a few not-soproud moments on the diamond with partners who fail to live up to our standards as umpires.

Chapter 6

Hey, Blue!

"Hey, Blue!"

We hear it all the time. "Hey, Blue, what's the count?" "Hey, Blue, you missed that call!" On and on it goes.

We get called "Blue" because our shirts are typically either navy blue or powder blue, and our hats are blue. If we wear jackets, they are blue as well. The pants we wear are, in most cases, a shade of gray.

We hear "Blue" more than we hear "Ump."

During one youth game, I heard "Hey, Blue" and I wished I hadn't.

This particular game happened to be one of the worst games ever played in the history of this wonderful sport. There was a varying combination of abilities. There were a few decent players, a group of below-average players, and the rest, who were there because mom or dad wanted them on the team to get exercise.

In this type of game, there is a one-man umpire system. The play is so slow and sloppy at times that a number of umpires feel that the coaches of the teams should be umpires in these games. It can be a waste of time for us, even though we get paid about thirty dollars a game to umpire. In fact, I compare it to a gym class softball game. It is not very competitive, and not very well-played.

During this game, it was quite apparent that the pitchers were struggling to get the ball across the plate, which is fairly normal for this league and this age group. Due to the pitchers' problems, I decided to let them pitch illegally, just so we could get through the game.

The pitchers physically were not able drag their back feet along the ground, which is required during delivery. One coach was furious about this, and he let me know it.

From his third base coaching box, he kept making critical remarks to me, and eventually I had to confront him. I walked to the third base box and I told him the reason for what I was doing. Our conversation was quiet, so only the two of us could hear. I was hoping that he would understand my rationale. Unfortunately, he did not, and he was furious.

"I showed her what she had to do with her back foot," I said to him, "but she's physically unable to do it. So for us to have a game, I'm going to let it go."

The coach was so angry that steam could have been coming from his ears.

"That is illegal," he said to me, as I walked away.

For the remainder of the game, I saw him turn to his team's fans, sitting near and behind the dugout. I heard him say to one fan, "He's going to let her pitch illegally. I can't believe it."

Keep in mind, this pitcher barely could get the ball across the plate. If she had been retiring hitters at a rapid pace with rise balls and fastballs, I would have called illegal pitches, resulting in a ball on the batter.

To add to the coach's frustration, his team lost. Before the teams went through the handshake line, he made his way directly to me, confronting me at the backstop as I got my timer and drink before leaving the field. He was now a few inches from my face.

"She pitched illegally all game. She did it last week, too," he barked at me.

"The game is over," I said. "I told you why I allowed it."

I immediately walked away, hoping to exit the field.

That's when I heard a voice from several yards away, "Hey, Blue!"

From the corner of my eye, I saw a fan sprinting toward me across the infield. He stopped me near the first base line. He appeared to be in his mid to late 30s, and he was full of wisdom to share.

"Hey, Blue, I want to show you this," he said, quickly pulling out his smartphone. This was one of the fans that the angry coach had been talking to during the game.

"I took some video of their pitcher during the game, and I want to show you what she was doing wrong," he said, fumbling to find the video on his device.

At this point, I was very upset. "I'm not going to watch that," I said as I walked away.

He then exploded. "That's why you don't know what you're doing!"

Several fans, probably stunned by this fan's willingness to confront me on the field after a game, witnessed that brief exchange. I exited the diamond by the first base dugout as fast as I could, and made my way to my vehicle to change clothes. At this point, a number of thoughts were racing through my mind, including, "I can't believe that just happened," and "They just should be lucky to have someone umpire one of their horrid games."

I like to view myself as someone who has lots of patience and can take most situations in stride, but I was stewing with anger that entire evening when I got home. Later that night, I debated long and hard about whether I should continue to umpire these lower-level recreation games.

I eventually relented, and decided that I would, indeed, umpire in this league in the future.

The behavior of this fan needed to be dealt with by league leadership. I contacted them following the game.

In this day and age, when a parent or spectator runs on the field after a game, an umpire starts to think he or she is being attacked. I know that thought definitely crosses my mind.

In addition, fans should not be trying to show umpires videos of the game on their smartphone before, during or after a game. How crazy is that? This is recreational youth softball. YOUTH SOFTBALL!!!

There are rights and wrongs in youth sports, and one of them always should be that fans should not be permitted on the ball diamond before, during or following a game. No exceptions.

Fans entering the field to confront a coach or umpire might end up sparking an ugly incident that ends up on the news.

You just never know what might happen.

Chapter 7

Expect the unexpected

My dad umpired blooper-ball back in the early 1960s. One time, he was the umpire for a game that would determine the league championship.

He made an "out" call to end the game at home plate. It was a split second call. The team that lost the game was furious. Emotions were soaring as my dad left the field.

After the game, one of the losing players got in his car and followed my dad to our house. The player confronted my dad in front of our house about his call, and the player wanted my dad to admit that he made the wrong call.

Fortunately, the debate did not get physical or out of hand. The player eventually left and went home.

This shows of how heated things can get during, as well as, after a game. This incident shows also how ridiculously players, coaches and fans can react and behave in recreation leagues at all levels of play.

One of my fellow umpires shared with me that he keeps a metal pipe in his vehicle just in case he is physically attacked by an irate player or spectator following a game. To my knowledge, he has yet to use it, but he is dead serious about having protection in case matters get out of hand. Umpires can face all kinds of nerve wracking situations.

Umpires sometimes have vulgar language used at them, are threatened, bullied and ridiculed. This can happen before, during or after a game. Every umpire has a story to tell when it comes to fan or player misbehavior. Some umpires can accept this part of the job, others can't. This is partly why it is so hard to get rookies into umpiring. At this time, the average age for an ASA umpire in Michigan is 55. Let's be honest, who wants to be the object of scorn on ball diamond, especially when you could be at home enjoying an iced tea on the back deck?

A few summers ago, shortly after a men's league game, an umpire from my area was almost hit by a beer can, thrown by an angry adult player. This is just one incident of many. If you do a Google search with the words "softball umpire attacked," you'll find several stories from all across the country about umpires getting punched or worse.

Every umpire's worst nightmare is that things can get heated and out of control in the blink of an eye.

One time, I was umpiring a game by myself in what I thought would be a fairly innocent game. It was toward the end of the season. Both teams (consisting of eighth-graders, I believe) were ending the season, and there were not any league championship at stake.

Working as a one-man crew has its advantages and disadvantages. On the positive side, you're making all the decisions on the field. It forces you to be assertive and to take charge of the game. On the negative side, you're all by yourself. There's no one there to have your back if things get dicey.

In this game, an assistant coach on one of the teams was not there to be an instructor or even to be supportive of the kids. He was there to be a pain in my neck.

He was a dad. I'm guessing him he was in his early 40s. He was kind of rough-looking. He had a bitter attitude toward umpires in general.

He was the first base coach for the team, and every time I called a pitch a "ball" or "strike" and he didn't like the call, he verbalized his mean-spirited thoughts. He unleashed one snarky comment after another. "Don't worry," he said to one batter after I called a strike. "I would not have swung at that either. No one would. That was a terrible call."

I gave the man a little bit of freedom to start the game, but soon, I had had enough. I told him to stop the comments and just coach his team.

That plan worked for about two minutes. He made another derogatory comment directed at me. That is when I told him that he was restricted to the dugout for the rest of the game, and that I had better not hear him say another word. He sheepishly headed to the dugout.

To start the next inning, his team was in the field. During warm-ups, his team's catcher turned to me and said something. I couldn't hear her, so I asked her to repeat it. She looked up at me and said, "Why couldn't you have restricted him to a place behind the bleachers?"

I chuckled to myself.

"You mean he's like that all the time?" I asked her.

She rolled her eyes and nodded "Yes."

When the game ended, the teams shook hands and I went to get my keys and drink. I passed by that assistant coach and he got in one last jab, "Nice game, Little League ump."

I didn't respond. I went to my vehicle to change out of my uniform and gear. A few minutes later, I saw this coach with one of his buddies leaving the field, and this guy was yelling at me with more comments. I was by myself. I was prepared for the worst.

The men were about 40 yards away, and I thought they were going to approach me at my vehicle. No one else was near me.

I started wondering what I was going to do if they got a few feet from me. What if this gets physical? Should I fight them? Should I call the police?

Thankfully they never did approach me. But later that night, I reported the incident to my supervisor, and I did a lot of thinking about how to handle potentially explosive situations in the future. I felt threatened that night because I thought it was going to get physical.

During training, we are instructed to call "9-1-1" in threatening situations, but what if a player or fan or coach is right in front of you and gets physical with you? Then what should you do? You can't tell them to wait a second so you can call the 9-1-1.

As umpires, we sometimes encounter these volatile situations. All of us have a fear of behavior getting out of hand. We watch the news. We see the reports of a disgruntled fan or coach attacking an umpire or sports official. For this reason, a number of states, including Michigan, have specific laws to punish those who assault sports officials.

It is the unpleasant side of what we do. We have to be aware of our circumstances at all times to avoid potentially explosive situations. Fortunately for us, the good times far outweigh the bad.

Chapter 8

Coaches, good and bad

Good coaches are easy to spot.

They are well-organized, knowledgeable about the rules, and positive people.

Generally speaking, teams of good coaches reflect that approach in the way they play the game. They play with a purpose. They know what they're doing on the field. The team is confident and upbeat.

Conversely, bad coaches are easy to spot, too. They tend to be disorganized, not rules-savvy, ill-tempered and they generate a feeling among the team that is negative.

The difference between these two types of coaches was never so apparent than when I umpired an ASA state tournament a few years ago.

In one dugout, there was the upbeat, positive coach who said a lot of encouraging words to his team. The players high-fived each other, shouted words of encouragement, and celebrated each other's successes.

In the other dugout, there were three fathers of players on the team leading the team as coaches. They were intense, hyper, harsh, and edgy. Guess how their team played the game?

This 16-and-under game started at eight o'clock in the morning, and by 8:05, I had my first face-to-face encounter with one of the edgy coaches.

He said that I had made the wrong call at second base on a steal. I thought I had made the right call. The father/coach did not agree. He gave me the stare-down treatment, with his eyes locked on mine for what seemed like a minute, but was only a few seconds. He was being a bully, trying to intimidate me.

This confrontation set the tone for the rest of the game.

Every close call was intensely challenge by one of their coaches. I began to feel as though nothing was going to make them happy.

In their dugout, this harsh demeanor was quite evident, too. The coaches got on the players for every mistake that they made. The players did not cheer for each other, there was not any celebrating, and there were not any smiles, ever, in that dugout.

The previous day, this team was almost involved in an on-field altercation after a player collided with the catcher at home plate. This team had a well-earned reputation for being poor sports.

Over on the other side of the field, the dugout atmosphere was just the opposite. Sure, it was a close game, but the other team had a positive spirit with cheering, clapping, and encouragement.

The positive team ended up winning the game by a couple of runs.

As I exited the field, the thought that went through my mind was this: "I would never want my daughter to play for those negative, demeaning coaches. What a terrible experience that would be."

Coaches can be that way in the lower age groups, as well. In fact, it could be worse. The expectations are often unrealistic.

At the young age groups, some parents still think that their daughter is going to go on to play for the University of Michigan or Florida or Arizona. If she's a good player at age ten, that means she'll be a super-star at eighteen or nineteen, right? Well, that unfortunately, is not the way it works.

A select few of these girls continue to play in later years. Some girls just leave the sport because they get tired of playing. Some girls meet their playing level ability peak at twelve or fourteen years of age. Some girls just choose to do other things. Most girls, to be brutally honest, just don't have the God-given talent that it takes to play in college.

One girl who probably is now choosing to do other things than softball is a girl I saw play for a ten and under travel team. Her dad was the coach, and, quite frankly, he just did not know how to coach.

He has to be given credit for volunteering his time to do this, and for giving up his summer, but the man just did not have the leadership skills to lead young kids. He was a poor fit.

His team was playing a game against a clearly much better opponent, which was well-organized, disciplined and had better athletes.

This coach's daughter was subbed into the game, where she played in leftfield. A ball was hit to her, she fielded it, and then she didn't know where to throw. She was confused. Base runners were hustling around the bases, and she hesitated. She ended up throwing the ball to the pitcher.

Her dad exploded in the dugout. He asked me to call timeout, and I did. He walked to the pitcher's circle, and yelled to his daughter, "C'mon. I'm taking you out of the game. You know that you're supposed to throw that ball to second base."

He pulled her from the game. As she ran in from leftfield, she started sobbing, and she continued to sob in the dugout and for the remainder of the game. It was a heart-breaking sight. This girl was either in the third or fourth grade, probably still playing with Barbies when she was at home.

If I could have thrown a coach out of a game for being a fool, I would have at this point. He had crushed his daughter's spirit in front of a large contingent of softball fans. She was embarrassed. I felt terrible for her.

As an umpire, I knew that I had to keep my mouth shut and my thoughts to myself in this case. It is not an umpire's business when it comes to how a person chooses to coach … and that's doubly true when it involves a coach's child.

For this reason, I so appreciate positive coaches who know what they are doing. This is not only true from an umpire's perspective, but also from that of a father whose own daughter plays softball.

Chapter 9

Parents

Every umpire has a story about parents. Do you know why? It is easy to pick on parents.

Most sports-minded moms and dads have the reputation of being overzealous, overprotective and unrealistic about their child's athletic prowess.

Years ago, one coach told me a classic story about dealing with parents after his team had just won a state championship in high school softball.

The championship was won on a Saturday morning. Later that same afternoon, a father of one of the players on the winning team visited the head coach at his house. Why? In order to complain about his daughter not batting high enough in the lineup in the state title game.

"His daughter started in the state championship game, and he was mad at me because she batted seventh in the order," the coach told me.

That story has stuck with me for 30 years.

Another veteran coach once half-jokingly confided to me that his dream job was to coach at an orphanage. That way, he said he wouldn't have to deal with know-it-all parents.

Indeed, some parents are really demanding and hard to please. But there also are very supportive and level-headed parents, as well. It's a mixed bag, in most cases, in youth and high school sports.

To be honest, my opinion of parents has evolved through the years. Before becoming a father, I was much harsher and much more critical of parents and their behavior at games. Once my wife and I became parents, I chilled out, and I was not as critical. I became more understanding because now I knew first-hand that emotions can be so powerful when your child is involved in the situation. I have lost my own cool at my daughter's sporting events, and I regretted it moments later. Sometimes angry and frustrated feelings take over for parents. It is tough to just walk away and shut up when you have a child involved in a game. That emotional attachment between a parent and the child is strong, and sometimes explosive.

For the most part, parents have treated me, as an umpire, very well at the youth and high school levels. Sure, they may get frustrated with a call and say something to me, but I just view that as part of the game. I can recall many times when a parent would offer me a bottle of water or ask if I needed to step into the shade of their umbrella on a hot day. That is cool stuff. I like that.

I have never threatened to kick a fan out of a game. One time, though, I felt like telling a fan to move from behind the backstop to a place in the outfield or even farther away, such as the parking lot.

This man happened to be a very large man, probably weighing close to four hundred pounds. He had a loud booming voice. He would never need a microphone in his life, even if he was a public address announcer at the Big House in Ann Arbor. His voice just carried.

His daughter was playing in a junior varsity game that was attended by only about twenty fans on a chilly Saturday morning. This dad sat in the bleachers about ten feet behind me. He sat in the front row.

He was repeatedly telling his daughter what to do.

"Keep your elbow up."

"Level off your swing."

"Hit a pitch in your zone."

Then, if she happened to hit the ball, he would yell at her to "run" as fast as she could. It should be noted that she was built like him. She lumbered to first base, and would get thrown out by ten feet. Then, he would get mad at her for being thrown out.

About midway through the game, I thought about getting earplugs from my vehicle. He was not doing anything illegal or inappropriate, except for irritating me with all the comments directed toward his daughter, which is not addressed in the rulebook.

I just had to tune him out as much as I could. As umpires, we often spot how parents interact with their son or daughter. We see the good, the bad and the ugly.

As for myself, when that day ended with the fan sitting behind the screen, I drove home in complete silence. I didn't want to hear any noise. I had heard enough from the Big Man Sitting Behind the Backstop.

Chapter 10

Dealing with the elements

One year in early April, I worked a Saturday tournament where the temperatures reached almost ninety degrees. It was a shock to the system.

No one in Michigan is prepared to face a day like that after you've been fighting through a cold winter. But then it happens – a freak day of hot weather.

I prepared for it the best way I knew how by drinking a lot of water, wearing short-sleeved umpire shirts, and being conservative in my movement. Most of my preparations were just common-sense.

Soon, the weather would take a turn for the worse. It happens that way in Michigan. One hot weekend might be followed up by fifty degree temperatures, or worse.

That is what happened in the spring of 2012.

After that sizzling day, I worked a doubleheader several days later, and it felt like it was mid-February. The wind was howling. The sky was gray. The temperature was about forty-five degrees. It was terrible.

Getting ready for game days like that was like getting ready to go winter camping. I dressed in layers. On that day in Midland, I dressed in five layers, a record for me.

Still, the wind was relentless. There was no escaping it. I could not get warm. I jumped up and down. I ran short sprints. I clapped my hands. I did anything and everything to keep moving, trying to generate body heat.

A few hours later, around 8 p.m., the double-header ended. I was numb, and so was my partner. We had survived a trip to the Tundra, and lived to tell about it.

That is when you turn the heat on "high" in your vehicle and just sit there for several minutes to thaw out before heading home.

That was not the worst day, however. My worst day was in Pinconning, a small town which is a short drive from Saginaw Bay and Lake Huron. On that April day, the wind was coming from the bay, and there was no protection to block it. There were not any buildings or trees. There were just open farm fields.

As the strong winds began to howl, snow flurries started to spit from the sky. We did not stop the game, though. We kept it going. Eventually, the flurries began to increase, and before we knew it, we had a brief blizzard on our hands.

Due to the blizzard-like conditions, we suspended the game, and the teams huddled in their dugouts with blankets, and anything else that would keep them warm. They were clumped together like one big mass of humanity.

Several minutes later, we resumed the game. The snow stopped, and the wind died down. We finished that doubleheader as fast as we could. Everyone wanted to get off the field in record time. Looking back on that winter-like day, I should have made that a six-layer day.

I cannot imagine what it would be like to umpire in northern Minnesota or any other far northern state, or, at the other extreme, how about Arizona or Texas or Florida in May, June and July when the temps are in the 90s or 100s? That would be brutal.

If you layer, you can always take clothes off, but when it is hot, you have to leave on what you are wearing. Just make sure to bring a lot of water, a cooling towel, and keep the air conditioner running when you are in the car.

Chapter 11

Battered and Bruised

Do you know when it is the most fun for me to be on the diamond? It is when I am officiating high-level talent.

I have been fortunate in my career to umpire games that included young ladies who went from the high school level to play college ball at the Division I, II and III levels.

I have been behind the plate for high school pitchers who not only were named All-League, but All-State. They throw heaters and changeups. They can throw rise balls and drop balls. I umpired the game of one pitcher who had the best curveball that I have ever seen. This pitch started at the right-handed hitter's waist, and then the ball would dip across the plate for a strike. It was awesome.

The best part, though, is that all of the pitchers are deadly accurate. That is what generally separates these pitches apart from other pitchers. If a strike is needed, they can throw a strike. If they want to miss on the outside corner by a few inches, then that is what they will do.

It is an absolute thrill to be behind the plate for these types of games.

At the lower levels of play, an umpire can encounter very good pitchers, as well, but if you have an All-Star pitcher, you also want to have an All-Star catcher in front of you.

If you do not, trouble could be brewing.

This age-old truth came to life one summer day in a 13-and-under game. Again, I was by myself. Again, I was eager to umpire a very good pitcher.

In this particular game, the catcher was not an All-Star. In fact, at the manager's meeting, the team's coach was pretty honest with me.

"My regular catcher will not be here until later. So the girl who is catching has never caught before," he said, before heading back to the dugout.

I stood several feet from the catcher as the pitcher - tall, lean and strong - hummed her warm-up pitches to the plate. The catcher caught one, and missed four, a couple of which hit her glove and deflected to the backstop. Now, I was worried.

I got behind the plate, pointed to the pitcher, and shouted, "Play." The first pitch was delivered to the plate, and this young and inexperienced catcher, somehow, caught the ball. The next several pitches did not have good accuracy, so the balls zipped past both the catcher and me. I felt like we were playing dodgeball.

One pitch zoomed past my leg. Another whistled past my shoulder. I stepped out from behind the plate, and for a moment, I thought about calling timeout to talk to the manager about changing catchers, or having myself stand behind the pitcher to call balls and strikes.

This was ridiculous, and it was getting dangerous. I got hit by one ball after it deflected off the catcher's mitt, and I responded by moving another few feet toward the backstop, so I would have more time to react. At this point, I was not concerned about proper mechanics. All I could think about was keeping me from being injured.

"You all right?" one coach asked me after I got hit.

"Yeah, I'm fine," I said, rubbing my sore arm.

To start the third inning, I heard those magic words. "Hey, Blue," the team's coach called to me. He then walked up to me, only a few feet away. "Our regular catcher is here. She will be behind the plate the next inning."

I just about fainted in relief.

The regular catcher got behind the plate, and I felt like I had a brick wall in front of me. She was strong, athletic, and skilled. I was no longer in harm's way.

After the game, I headed over to where I parked and where the other umpires park their vehicles. We sat and talked, as is typical at most ball parks following a night of games.

I asked one of the umpires, Dave, if he had ever worked one of the "Orange team's" games, which was the color of the shirts of the team which had the lethal pitcher and not-so-good backup catcher.

"Yeah, I had them last week," he said.

"Did you get hit by any pitches? I was umping behind a catcher who couldn't catch, and their pitcher could really throw hard," I said.

He paused for a second, and finally said. "I got hit twenty-eight times."

He proceeded to point to his wrist, elbow, shoulder and other parts of his body. Each time, he would say, "I got hit here, here, here …"

We shared a smile.

"I know exactly what you are talking about," I said. "I caught a break. Their regular catcher ended up showing up in the third inning."

"Well, she did not show up for my game," he replied.

We are well-protected in our plate gear. Still, those balls hurt when you get hit. I had a foul-tip once hit me squarely in the chest protector, and it stung for the rest of the inning. I have been hit in the forearm, hands, neck area, and I have had foul-tips knock my mask off my face.

Like other umpires, I have had bruises that lasted for days, if not weeks.

As an umpire, you learn to take your lumps, bumps, and bruises, and move on to the next game.

Chapter 12

Striking out my daughter

One of the biggest reasons that I decided to get into umpiring girls fast-pitch softball is that I have two daughters. At the time that I started umpiring fast-pitch, they were pretty young, so I was not sure what sport they might choose to participate in.

I was hoping it would be softball. I have always enjoyed the game. I used to play slow-pitch and modified in my younger days. As a sportswriter, I have covered games at the highest level possible -- world tournaments. I have also reported on games at the high school and college levels. One summer, the USA Women's Olympic team visited our city, and I watched the great Jennie Finch pitch against an area All-Star team in an exhibition game.

I had a lot of experience being around the game.

As a father of girls, I wanted to get myself prepared if one of my daughters decided to play softball. My younger daughter, Ellie, eventually did start playing at the age of nine in the local recreation league.

I loved going to her games, and I made sure that I would not be umpiring on those nights. I "blocked" my schedule so I would not get any assignments, and that typically worked out perfectly. It was a nice, relaxing night.

I just wanted to be a dad on those nights. My wife and I, along with our daughter, Nahomie, sat in our lawn chairs several feet from the backstop, and offered encouraging words to Ellie and her teammates.

One game night, the teams were warming up and I started to look around for the umpire. None was in sight. In ten-and-under recreation play, there is one umpire for each game and the umpire is usually a high school-aged student.

As game time approached, the coaches met at home plate and started to talk. The umpire had yet to make an appearance. Then, I saw them look at me. I knew what was coming.

Adam, the coach of my daughter's team, slowly strolled to the backstop, and politely asked me, "Would you mind umpiring our game if our umpire does not show up?"

My mind went blank for a few seconds. I never wanted to umpire one of my daughter's games. I just wanted to be a dad.

I couldn't say no. They needed an umpire to have a game, so I told Adam that I would umpire the game, but I would do it from behind the circle because I didn't have my plate gear. He agreed to my request.

Once my daughter, Ellie, figured out what was going on, I could hear her in the dugout, excitedly telling her teammates, "My daddy's going to be the umpire! My daddy's going to be the umpire!"

The game eventually started, and I took my position behind the pitcher. Things were going smoothly. No questionable plays. Nothing out of the ordinary was happening.

Then, my daughter walked to the plate to bat. Instantly, I thought, "I hope she gets a hit. I don't want to call out my own daughter on strikes."

My daughter was not an aggressive hitter. Like a lot of girls that age, she liked to look for a walk. Sure enough, the pitcher had good control and was able to throw strikes.

Ellie worked the count to 3-2. The next pitch would decide her fate.

The pitcher delivered the pitch, and my daughter did not swing. She watched the ball go by and sink snuggly into the catcher's mitt.

"Strike three," I yelled.

As Ellie slowly headed back to the dugout, she turned to look at me, and shrugged her shoulders, and I shrugged mine.

Later during the car ride home, I told her, "Ellie, I never want to strike out my daughter again."

I got paid twenty dollars to work that game, and from that point on, I have never umpired another one of my daughter's games.

Chapter 13

Privacy

As umpires, we like our privacy.

Fans should not park where umpires park or invade our turf on game days.

That is just the way it is, and, truthfully, the way it should be.

Parking is crucial. Umpires like to be separated from the fans.

From my perspective, I like knowing that there is an "umpires only" parking area when I am working a weekend tournament.

The isolation is necessary because it gives us a chance to be ourselves and to talk freely. We can talk about rules and plays that we have encountered. We can talk about difficult players and coaches. We can take naps, read, eat a lunch and not be disturbed. If we are so inclined, we can have peace and quiet before our next game. Simply, we can be at peace.

The last thing that I want is for a fan to approach me at my vehicle, asking about a rule or what happened in a prior game. I have never hung out a "Do Not Disturb" sign, but I probably should.

We also are very cautious in how we dress on game days.

At a typical weekend tournament in the summer, I will work anywhere from three to five games in a day. I may have a game at 8:30 in the morning, then another at 11 a.m., 3 p.m. and 6 p.m.

What an umpire does between games is important. We are encouraged to get out of our umpire gear and attire as quickly as possible, and change into "regular" clothes, such as dress shorts and a T-shirt.

The reason for this is pretty obvious. We do this so that the fans will not recognize us as an umpire if we walk around the complex, go to the concession stand, or head to the restroom.

Once at a tournament in Mount Pleasant, I worked a game that was pretty intense. The losing team's coach was not happy with my performance that day, and he let me know about it before exiting the field.

Soon, I headed to where the umpires parked so I could change out of my clothes and into dress shorts, a T-shirt, and sandals. I always wear a ball-cap, too, and sunglasses, which add to my disguise.

After I got something to eat from my cooler, I went to use the restroom. Guess who was in the men's room? You guessed it - the angry coach who was not happy with me.

I stood right next to him at the sink. He washed his hands, and looked into the mirror. I recognized him, but he didn't recognize me.

He quickly glanced at me, but that was it. He just left without saying a word. I assume he didn't know who I was. If he did, he sure didn't show it and react to my presence.

Without fail, I will change as quickly as humanly possible after my game is completed. So far, I have not been recognized when out of uniform.

I hope it stays that way.

Chapter 14

Getting serious

At some point in the budding career of an umpire, a decision has to be made.

How far do I want to go with my umpiring experience?

Some are content umpiring in the recreation leagues, and maybe an occasional high school game. Others like to do everything – recreation, high school and college, if possible. An umpire can make decent money umpiring just in recreational leagues and high school, with some ambitious umpires exceeding five thousand dollars for a spring and summer season. It all depends on how many games that you want to work. The more games that you work, the more money you can earn.

Heading into the 2016 season, I decided it was time to increase my umpiring time. I was really enjoying the work. I loved being around the game, and my confidence was really growing.

I was confident in my knowledge of the rules, which is absolutely crucial in becoming a respected umpire. That may seem like overstating the obvious, but it is the truth. There is nothing worse than an umpire who doesn't know the rules or who struggles to communicate a rule to an inquiring coach or player. It makes the umpire crew look foolish.

You do not want to appear uncertain at explaining a rule or call. You want to be viewed as someone with authority. The only way to learn the rules is to study the rulebook. That's an absolute nonnegotiable in becoming a good umpire. I read the rulebook, and looked at umpiring videos on YouTube to pick up tips. I was becoming a student of umpiring.

To increase my knowledge, if a college softball game was on TV, I would watch the umpires and not the players. If I had an off day, I would go and watch a local high school game, always watching what the umpires did. I studied what they did, when they did it and how they did it. I was looking for tips to apply when I was on the field.

I practiced my mechanics and techniques at home, sometimes looking in the mirror to watch how my arm was positioned for a strike call – right arm extended above the shoulder, fist clenched. I practiced my "strike" and "out" calls as a way to have good voice command. I practiced my "strike three" call. It is important to do things the right way on a consistent basis.

To set the stage for a successful season in 2016, I decided to attend a national umpire clinic in Lake Orion, north of Detroit. This clinic was sponsored by the highly-respected ASA organization, which hosts a number of state and national tournaments for men and women throughout the nation.

Not only did I want to learn more by attending this clinic, but I wanted to get my name out there and network. I wanted the ASA leadership to know that I was serious about umpiring.

From Friday to Sunday, I attended several sessions to improve my mechanics and positioning. I felt good, really good, in understanding what was being taught and why we needed to do things a certain way.

When that weekend ended, I was ready for action. It was like going to spring training, and getting prepared for the upcoming regular season.

The high school season was about to start in April, and I had a full schedule of junior varsity and varsity games assigned to me.

I felt that I was on top of my game. I was not perfect, far from it, but I was very confident on the field – in everything from dealing with players and coaches, to knowing and applying the rules, to proper positioning, and communicating with my partner. Just like in a good marriage, communication is essential on the field among umpires.

"I am at third, John," I might say to my partner. Or I might say, "I have the tag." Without fail, you want to communicate at all times, particularly when things appear to be a bit confusing on the field.

It is crucial to let your partner know what is going on, and where you plan to be. Umpires need to trust each other. That trust is built on communication. We refer to ourselves as the "third team on the field" because, like the teams competing between the lines, we need to work as a team, too.

My high school season went great. I umpired a number of good teams, including a pair of teams that ended up playing for a state championship in Division 4.

By the end of May, my high school season was wrapping up, and I was eagerly anticipating June and July, and the opportunity to work local league games and some weekend tournaments, including an ASA state tournament in Mount Pleasant.

It was turning out to be a great 2016 season.

Chapter 15

In a groove

Bologna sandwiches, lots of fruit, granola bars, and a vast supply of water and grape Powerade. What do all of these have in common?

This is what typically fills my cooler when I head out to umpire a weekend tournament. I refrain from soda pop, fast food and sweets. They make me sluggish, and I cannot afford to be sluggish when I am on the field.

I want to feel energetic, but most of all, I want to be well nourished and hydrated. I never want to run out of water to drink, especially during a hot summer afternoon in June or July. Those days can absolutely drain you. The sun is hot, and typically there is not any shade on most diamonds, so I coat myself generously with sunscreen to keep from doing damage to my skin.

I cannot even imagine how many calories I burn during a typical tournament day, when I am working four games in the hot sun. All I know is that it is extremely important to drink a lot of fluids so I do not get dehydrated. This precaution is an absolute must. I've known umpires who've collapsed due to heat exhaustion. The heat can be brutal.

The summer of 2016 brought two highlights.

My first was working in a state ASA tournament, which typically attracts dozens of the state's best softball travel teams from age 18-U down to 10-U. I spent the first night in a dormitory on the campus of Central Michigan University in Mount Pleasant. Umpires could stay in the rooms for free, but after spending one sleepless night in the dorm, I decided to head back home for the next two nights. It was only a forty minute drive, so that was very feasible, even after umpiring three or four games and being pretty exhausted at the end of the day.

I had an awesome crew at my designated field on Broomfield Road. You never know who is going to be assigned to your fields, but in this case, everything worked out great. No worries.

I umpired with a number of people whom I was meeting for the very first time. Fortunately we all clicked.

The games were well played. The hassles were few. I got a chance to umpire an 18-U game that featured an excellent pitcher who had been named the freshman pitcher of the year in her college's conference. That was a treat. Like I said before, anytime that you get a chance to umpire the plate for a great pitcher, it's extremely special, almost an honor. It was my privilege to work her game.

When the tournament wrapped up, I had worked nine games, and had earned two hundred seventy dollars, which averaged out to thirty dollars a game. It had been a good paying weekend.

The thing that separates the ASA state tournament apart from other tournaments is that it is run very efficiently, and umpires are evaluated for their work throughout the tournament, both on the field and behind the plate. Umpires are judged on positioning, execution of calls, how they dress, proper mechanics and game management. It is a thorough evaluation, and one that I always look forward to reading when it arrives in the mail a few weeks later.

I was thrilled when I got my evaluation after the Mount Pleasant tournament. I received very good marks from my field supervisor. I was quite encouraged.

I felt as though this tournament was one of my better tournaments. When I was out of position, I knew it. When I did not process a situation quickly, I knew that as well. I was able to quickly fix my mistakes, and then move on to the next play. This is the way you are supposed to operate as an umpire.

My confidence was soaring as I worked the following weekend in Grand Blanc, near Flint, in a tournament that is called a "College Showcase." College softball coaches are encouraged to attend this tournament to eye some of the state's best talent in a variety of age groups. There are a lot of quality teams on display for the entire weekend.

During this tournament, one play stood out for me. The game was close, and the home team was trailing by two runs in the bottom of the seventh inning.

The home team rallied to cut the deficit to one. With the potential tying and go-ahead runners on first and second and two outs, a batter hit a slow roller to the shortstop, who made a great play to field the ball and threw it to first base.

From my position behind the shortstop, I called the girl out at first base to end the game. It was incredibly close, and if I had called her safe, the team would have had the bases loaded.

I could hear a loud groan from the crowd. The home team's fans thought she was safe. I definitely could understand how they felt. It was a bang-bang call.

As I headed toward the dugout to get my water and leave the field, a very large man stood against the fence. Like a big grizzly bear, he growled at me and said, "You missed that call." He stood about 6-foot-6 and was built like a football player. I believe he was the father of the girl whom I called out at first base.

I looked up at him, and said nothing. I just left the field with my partner. I refuse to talk to parents following a game because it is not only frowned upon in the profession, but it typically leads to a debate. I am not interested in a discussion with a parent after a ballgame. I want to ignore them as much as possible.

When I got back to my vehicle, I did a lot of thinking about that call. Did I blow it? Was she safe? I finally just had to let it go and move on to the next game. That is an important practice in this business – learn to move on. If you do not, that added stress will give you ulcers.

As I finished my time at this tournament, I was approached by the director, Jeff Yorke, who told me that the state umpire-in-chief for ASA, Bryan Smith, wanted me to give him a call. I asked Jeff what it was about, and he said that he did not know for sure.

Sitting in my Trail Blazer, I called Bryan on my cellphone. He asked if I would be interested in working in a national tournament later in July. One was in Michigan, the other in Ohio. He was very enthusiastic about my work, and he wanted to reward me with a coveted assignment.

I checked out the dates and, sadly, I had to turn down both offers. The dates conflicted with my day job as a sports editor at the newspaper. I could not take the time off for vacation. There was too much was going on in Midland during those weekends.

"Sorry, Bryan, I cannot do it. But keep me in mind for next year."

I was looking forward to a fun and exciting 2017.

Chapter 16

Adversity

My high school assignments start coming in around the middle of December. By Christmas, I already had about five or six dates on my schedule for spring. More games would soon be available. I was getting excited about being on the diamond.

With games now on my calendar, I started to plot out my spring. I set a goal to work at least twenty high school dates, including some Saturday tournaments. After the high school season ended, I focused on a few tournaments in June and July before I shut down my schedule in August.

My umpiring year was starting to take shape.

I was determined to make this my best season yet. I planned to attend local and state clinics, and work a lot of games. I set a goal to work a national tournament, which I thought was a strong reality.

The plan was in place. I was getting pumped about the upcoming season. A healthy dose of anticipation helps to make a harsh Michigan winter go by faster.

Then I went to work on January 12, 2017.

That is when everything changed in the blink of an eye.

The date always will be etched in my mind until the day that I die. I drove to work early in the morning. The roads were icy due to freezing rain over night. I had to drive extremely carefully to get to work. When I got out of my vehicle, it was like walking on a skating rink --- only worse. It was extremely slippery.

I made it safely into the building at 6:30 in the morning. I performed my work duties, and then headed out for lunch shortly after 11 a.m. I decided to back-track through the building, because I thought that would be the safest and easiest route to my vehicle, which was parked on the street, about fifteen yards from our press room door.

As I opened that door, I looked down on the sidewalk, which led to my vehicle. The sidewalk was snow-covered. There was a gentle snow falling from the sky. It appeared to be just another winter day in Michigan.

I took two, maybe three steps on the sidewalk --- and my life instantly changed. My right foot shot out on the ice, which the snow was covering. My left leg violently contorted, and I felt an explosion in my left knee area. As sickening as it may sound, I could feel something being shredded in my knee. I fell to the ground, screaming in pain. It felt as though my kneecap had been shot off by a shotgun. I had never experienced such intense pain, and I hope to never experience it again.

Minutes later, I would be taken to the local hospital. I could not walk and I could not put any pressure at all on my left leg.

Originally, the diagnosis was a knee sprain. But I knew it was worse than that. A few days later, I was examined by a local orthopedic surgeon, David Bortel, who determined that I had ruptured my quadriceps tendon, a fairly rare, but serious injury.

He scheduled my surgery for January 23, 2017. The hour-long surgery was a success, but in order to fix my tendon, he had to attach it to my kneecap with an implant and two titanium screws. My left leg was useless, and I had zero strength. I could not lift my left leg, not even a centimeter.

The night of the surgery was intense. As I lay in bed at home, I thought about a lot of things: my job at the newspaper, my quality of life going forward, how I would survive a winter on only one leg, and how this would impact my ability to umpire.

I knew that I was in deep trouble. My doctor told me that I would be on crutches for at least four months, and I would have to wear a leg immobilizer for about the same length of time. In addition to this, there was the physical therapy, weeks upon weeks of physical therapy.

I then made the mistake of going online and researching recovery time for my type of injury and surgery. Needless to say, it was depressing. Some people who had gone through this surgery said it took them more than a year to get back to normal. Others said they were still struggling a year after their surgery.

I stopped looking at these forums because I had to keep my sanity and have some hope.

Despite the bleak odds, I was determined to umpire in the summer.

I was clinging to hope.

Chapter 17

Clinging to hope

I could not go to work. I was in bed most of the day. I needed help to get in and out of bed, and in and out of chairs.

Bluntly, I was in rough shape. This was a few weeks after the surgery.

My mind was starting to come out of the fog, and the thought of umpiring in the spring and summer of 2017 was fool's gold. I knew that I was incapable of umpiring.

How could I possibly umpire when I could not even walk? Well, the answer is that I was not capable of umpiring.

Dr. Bortel told me that it would be a very demanding recovery. Realistically, I was looking at five or six months to be able to walk normally again.

Determined, I told my physical therapists, "I want to be able to umpire again."

That was my goal, the carrot that I was chasing.

First, though, I had to let my high school game assignor, Brad Crampton, know that I would not be umpiring that spring, and that he should give my games to another umpire. I contacted Bryan Smith, the state umpire-in-chief, to let him know what had happened to me. I also contacted the local UIC, Jason Gehoski, to let him know my situation.

I was crossing names off my list. One by one, I was contacting umpires and tournament directors to let them know what had happened to me, and that I was going to miss the entire 2017 season.

Emotionally, I was OK. I wasn't angry or bitter. I just dealt with my circumstances the best way possible. I had a long road to recovery, and I needed to face it with courage, hope and optimism. There was no room for discouragement or pessimism.

A few weeks after contacting my fellow umpires and tournament directors, I received another piece of unexpected news in early April --- I lost my job as sports editor at the Midland Daily News. My position had been eliminated due to company restructuring. I had been there for more than thirty-three years, the last fifteen plus years as the sports editor. Now, I was injured and jobless.

I had been off of work since the mishap in January, so when I was told that my job was eliminated, that came via a phone call. In retrospect, that probably was a blessing in disguise. Since I had been off of work for a few months, I was somewhat detached from the job and all of my duties. Still, hearing those words is never easy, and it took me a while to process what had just happened to me.

With time on my hands, a number of people encouraged me to write a book. "A book about what?" I wondered to myself.

I thought about what I could write about for a long period of time. Then it came to me: write about something that I love and know first-hand.

So, I decided to write a first-person account of what it is like being an umpire in youth and high school softball. Writing an umpiring book is what I did to help fill my solitary days, and to keep my writing skills sharp. I was often alone during the day because my wife is a teacher and my daughters are in middle school. Writing helped me to occupy my days, so I daily got up at 7 in the morning to work on this book for a couple of hours at a time.

When I wasn't writing, I spent a lot of time pondering this uncertain period in my life. I thought long and hard about my circumstances, and two terms perfectly describe how I felt inside: grateful and at peace. That may seem very odd to some people, given my difficult circumstances, but it is the bottom-line truth. I had little to no anxiety throughout that period of time.

One of my favorite Bible verses is from James, chapter one, and it says to "consider it all joy" when you encounter various trials in life. That was my over-riding mindset. I thought about those verses on a daily basis, and I would tell my friends that those verses in James were my life-line. I viewed my circumstances as though God was directly involved, and that gave me an optimistic perspective on my future. He was going to successfully see me through this period of my life.

When my job loss became public, I was grateful for all the support and encouragement that I received from friends and those in the community. I received a large number of kind and thoughtful emails, text messages and Facebook posts. When I shed tears, it was only because I was overwhelmed by the responses from all the wonderful people who have rallied to my side, offering encouragement and hope, and kind words to help me get through my adversity.

As my recovery process still unfolds, I have to be brutally honest with myself: It is going to take a tremendous amount of work to get myself healthy and return to umpiring. Physical therapy is a tedious, long, and painstaking journey. Some days are very rough.

Even though I see improvement in my condition, as much as I try, I cannot picture myself working behind the plate, with my feet spread in their proper position, and me lowering my body for every pitch. Just the thought of that sends chills down my spine.

Quite frankly, my return to umpiring seems like it is a galaxy away at this point. That is what a serious injury like this does to the mind and body. It almost puts a person into a temporary fog.

Yet, as long as I continue to get healthier each day and each week, there is hope for a brighter tomorrow. That is what I choose to dwell on in my mind, and that is what I cling to each day as I go through rehabilitation. I may return to umpiring next year or I may not return until two or three years down the road when I'm in my late 50s, almost 60. Who knows? I certainly do not, although I am working hard to get my leg back to normal by walking, doing strengthening exercises and lifting weights. I want to be 100 percent when I step on the field. I never want to experience another injury like that ever again.

This has been quite the journey, not only recently with my job loss and injury, but also since the day that I became a fast-pitch umpire back in 2010. I have met a lot of great people, and I have been able to umpire countless softball games over the past several years. I do not want it to end prematurely due to an injury. I believe I still have more games left in me. I really do.

This adversity has forced me to do a lot of praying, and to trust God for my future. I chose to be grateful. That's my approach to my life's journey. With His help, I am determined to work hard to get my health back to 100 percent and return to the diamond as an umpire.

That is what keeps me motivated as I learn to walk, and eventually run, all over again.

Epilogue

Roughly six months after my surgery, I'm off of crutches and I don't have to wear a knee brace. I'm able to walk, but I still have trouble navigating steps. I go up and down stairs very cautiously because of the stress and pressure it puts on my left knee. My strength has improved in my leg thanks to all of the exercises that I do with my physical therapists, who have been fantastic. I also swim on a regular basis and work out at the gym to stay in shape. My hope is that by this coming winter I'll be able to jog or run on a treadmill. I'm not too excited about having to deal with another winter of ice, snow and cold after what happened to me last January. That's a mental hurdle that I'll need to clear. I live in Michigan, so I have to accept the fact that it will snow and be cold, but wintering in Florida sure seems more and more enticing as winter draws near. I can work on my rehabilitation in a nice climate, without having to deal with the winter elements (Florida doesn't have icy sidewalks, right?) I'm hopeful to step on the diamond next spring. That's my plan. And if I do, I'll be very grateful to hear those words, "Hey, Blue!"

About the author: Chris A. Stevens is a Michigan-based author and journalist, who spent more than 35 years in the newspaper business. He was twice named one of the top 10 sports columnists in the nation by the Associated Press Sports Editors in the category of circulations 30,000 and under. To purchase his Kindle ebook or print book, go to the book section of www.amazon.com

Made in the USA
Middletown, DE
29 June 2018